Printed in Great Britain
by Amazon

38145684R00056